MEET ME AT THE LIGHTHOUSE

ALSO BY DANA GIOIA

MEET ME AT THE LIGHTHOUSE

• • •

POEMS BY

Dana Gioia

Graywolf Press

This publication is made possible, in part, by the voters of Minnesota
through a Minnesota State Arts Board Operating Support grant, thanks
to a legislative appropriation from the arts and cultural heritage fund.
Significant support has also been provided by the McKnight Foundation,
the Lannan Foundation, the Amazon Literary Partnership, and other
generous contributions from foundations, corporations, and individuals.
To these organizations and individuals we offer our heartfelt thanks.

Published by Graywolf Press
212 Third Avenue North, Suite 485
Minneapolis, Minnesota 55401

www.graywolfpress.org

Published in the United States of America

ISBN 978-1-64445-215-8 (paperback)
ISBN 978-1-64445-216-5 (ebook)

2 4 6 8 9 7 5 3 1
First Graywolf Printing, 2023

Library of Congress Control Number: 2022938628

Cover design: Kyle G. Hunter

Cover art: Jason Leung / Unsplash

In memory of three generations

JESÚS ORTIZ
FRANCISCO ORTIZ
THEODORE ORTIZ

Let us praise the dignity of their destitution.

CONTENTS

I.

II.

III.

IV.

V.

MEET ME AT THE LIGHTHOUSE

· I ·

MEET ME AT THE LIGHTHOUSE

Meet me at the Lighthouse in Hermosa Beach,
That shabby nightclub on its foggy pier.
Let's aim for the summer of '71,
When all our friends were young and immortal.

I'll pick up the cover charge, find us a table,
And order a round of their watery drinks.
Let's savor the smoke of that sinister century,
Perfume of tobacco in the tangy salt air.

The crowd will be quiet—only ghosts at the bar—
So you, old friend, won't feel out of place.
You need a night out from that dim subdivision.
Tell Dr. Death you'll be back before dawn.

The club has booked the best talent in Tartarus.
Gerry, Cannonball, Hampton, and Stan,
With Chet and Art, those gorgeous greenhorns—
The swinging-masters of our West Coast soul.

Let the All-Stars shine from that jerry-built stage.
Let their high notes shimmer above the cold waves.
Time and the tide are counting the beats.
Death the collector is keeping the tab.

THE ANCIENT ONES

Why do they lie to us, the ancient ones,
whispering their fables by the fire?
Otherwise so glib and garrulous,
they answer not a word to our objections
but smugly nod at their own oracles.

Why do the children listen to the stories,
their rosy mouths agape, their eyes intent?
Who could enjoy such patchwork chronicles?
But when we mock their far-fetched climaxes,
they pay no heed and start another tale.

MAP OF THE LOST EMPIRE

Live long enough, and you become a Victorian,
part of you always dressed in black
like the Empress of India, mourning your lost ones
in Tennysonian cadences.

You study the map of your once vast empire
with its carefully engraved borders of vanished nations,
remembering the wide harbors and flag-filled capitals.
The sun never sets on your nostalgia.

What expeditions, what discoveries there were—
circling the volcano's sulphurous perimeter,
trekking the glacier, naming a new orchid
amid a chorus of blue frogs.

Now the volcano—long dormant—has a small café
reached by a comfortable funicular.
The cities you revisit are populated by strangers
dressed like American teenagers.

Such humiliating surrenders and abandonments!
Who is that ludicrous impostor in the mirror?
Where are the regiments to hold back the years?
What fortress left to make a stand?

PARDON ME, PILGRIM

To a luna moth

Pardon me, pilgrim. I forgot your name
When you arrived last night at our front door,
A baneful vagrant from the stormy skies,
Your broad wings marked with two ferocious eyes.

But your fierce gaze proved beauty in disguise.
A dusty sweetness under fictive eyes.
Giant of your fragile race, you came
By gusty happenstance and nothing more.

Yet still I wondered what had brought you here
So late when I, too, wandered aimlessly.
But mute with wonder, how could I inquire
The secrets of your lunar embassy?

TEDIUM

How elegant ennui once was, *mon cher*,
the suave satiety of Baudelaire—
memorious and metrical—who slowed
the jagged hours with absinthe and Pernod.
Lost is the life of languor and longueurs,
inactionable angers, and lechery
so soft, it will not rouse itself to feed.

The flies intone their imbecilic whir,
luxe, calme et volupté—love's rancid feast.
The poet has reclined in ecstasy,
dreaming of fame, surrounded by the tiers
of books he has not, will not ever read.
The flesh is sad, and boredom is a beast
that sprawls upon the rug and will not stir.

THREE DRUNK POETS

Do you remember where we were that night,
three of us, walking down a small-town street,
reciting poems from memory?

We would not turn around, we vowed,
until one of us ran out of poems. Some ideas
seem brilliant when you're blitzed.

First came the easy ones—Shakespeare,
Tennyson, Dickinson, Poe. Yeats
took most of a mile, Frost another.

We spoke in turns—Larkin and Kees,
Stevens, Millay—each poem a sort of confession.
"No more Millay!" our friend begged.

A passerby would've looked away embarrassed,
but we strode beaming like ambassadors
exchanging costly gifts.

The street became an empty country lane,
silvered by the moon. "Look!" you pointed back,
"We have outwalked the furthest city light."

Half a mile later, we reached Catullus,
and a coyote joined the contest.
"Where the hell are we?" groaned our friend.

By then it was nearly 3 a.m.,
and so we headed back to town—
walking in silence—still not sober.

TRAVEL

The queer thing is that I hate to travel.

To lean over the rail of an ocean liner
above the crowded dock as the gangway rises
and the blast horn bellows its throbbing farewell,
scattering the screeching gulls, and the great vessel
slides through the azure harbor to the open sea
is an experience I prefer to see on screen.

The images of holiday cruise buffets,
iced pyramids of rosy shrimp and crab claws,
slabs of smoked salmon, lattices of fresh cut cheese,
and aproned sous-chefs slicing pink roast beef
beside a steaming chowder pot, give me *mal de mer*.
I hunger most to quench my appetites.

While my workmates gush over colorful brochures,
enraptured by the enticing maps and menus
of easily affordable adventures—one click away—
I fantasize of staying at home alone,
free of the office, every phone and screen turned off,
sprawled on the couch with a book and mug of coffee.

Let someone else ascend the heights of Machu Picchu,
tramp through marshes terrifying the flamingos
or navigate the Gulf of Aden in a dhow.
I'm satisfied to get a postcard with a foreign stamp.
I feel no need to vacate my own existence.
Isn't the point to be happy where you are?

But so little in life is about being happy.

AT THE CROSSROADS

Here are the crossroads where old women come
Under the quarter moon to cast their spells,
And where young lovers meet to argue out
The secret terms of their surrender.

It is a place that each sees differently—
The salesman scouting, soldiers tramping home,
The scholar napping by the riverbank
While someone else's fortune drifts downstream.

But if you stand at crossroads long enough,
Most of the eager world comes strutting by—
Businessmen, preachers, cats—all going somewhere,
Even the Devil striking up a deal.

I used to wonder if they ever got there.
Be careful here in choosing where to turn.
You learn a lot by staying in one place
But never how the story truly ends.

SEAWARD

In memory of Theodore Ortiz,
US Merchant Marine

Kneel on the stones,
the sea commands.
Then cup your hands
in the shallow tide.
Quench your thirst
with stinging brine.
No taste more bitter
nor truer than mine.

Savor the blessings
of my refusal.
No argosy
will satiate
the hungers of
your restlessness.
No harbor house
your homelessness.

The empty lighthouse
flanks the sound,
mute memorial
to the drowned.
Stand on the dock
as the ocean swells.
Death is what happens
to somebody else.

TINSEL, FRANKINCENSE, AND FIR

Hanging old ornaments on a fresh cut tree,
I take each red glass bulb and tinfoil seraph
And blow away the dust. Anyone else
Would throw them out. They are so scratched and shabby.

My mother had so little joy to share
She kept it in a box to hide away.
But on the darkest winter nights—*voilà*—
She opened it resplendently to shine.

How carefully she hung each thread of tinsel,
Or touched each dime-store bauble with delight.
Blessed by the frankincense of fragrant fir,
Nothing was too little to be loved.

Why do the dead insist on bringing gifts
We can't reciprocate? We wrap her hopes
Around the tree crowned with a fragile star.
No holiday is holy without ghosts.

"WORDS, WORDS, WORDS"

It isn't just the words, though we have made
a science of them. Eloquence excels
in polishing the sentiments we need
no longer say.
Words are the cards, not why the game is played.

It isn't just the rhyme, though we surmise
the accidental insights of conjunction—
the superstitious chanting we despise
but can't forget,
shamed by our childish pleasure in surprise.

It isn't just the pain we hope to end.
Old wounds still seep their blood between the lines.
The truest words subvert what we intend.
They bring no ease.
The cost is always more than we can spend.

It is the luck to fail at what we started,
of letting language use us as a vessel
swept on a course we never could have charted—
to hope that once
the angel came, possessed us, and departed.

· II ·

Jesús Ortiz, July 1900.

THE BALLAD OF JESÚS ORTIZ

Jake's family were vaqueros.
They worked the cattle drives
Down from Montana to market.
They did what it took to survive.

Jake's real name was Jesús,
Which the Anglos found hard to take,
So after a couple of days,
The cowboys called him Jake.

When Jake was twelve, his father
Brought him along to ride.
"Don't waste your youth in the pueblo.
Earn by your father's side."

The days were hot and toilsome,
But all of the crew got fed.
It wasn't hard to sleep on the ground
When you've never had a bed.

Three thousand head of cattle
Grazing the prairie grass,
Three thousand head of cattle
Pushed through each mountain pass.

Three thousand head of cattle
Fording the muddy streams,
And then three thousand phantoms
Bellowing in your dreams.

At night when the coyotes called,
Jake would sometimes weep
Recalling how his mother
Sang her children to sleep.

But when he rose in the morning,
The desert air was sweet.
No sitting in a mission school
With bare and dusty feet.

And when the drive was over,
He got his pay—and then
He came back to the pueblo
Where he was one of the men.

Ten years on the open range
He led the vaquero's life,
Far from his home in Sonora,
No children and no wife.

Then Jake headed north to Wyoming
To find his winter keep
Among the Basques and Anglos
Who raised and slaughtered sheep.

He came to cold Lost Cabin
Where the Rattlesnake Mountains rise
Over the empty foothills,
Under the rainless skies.

The herders lived in dugouts
Or shacks of pine and tar.
The town had seven buildings.
The biggest was the bar.

John Okie owned the town,
The Sheep King of Wyoming.
He owned the herds. He owned the land
And every wild thing roaming.

He hired Jake for his tavern.
He let him sleep in the kitchen.
Mexicans worked hard
And didn't waste time bitching.

Tending bar was easier
Than tending cattle drives.
Jake poured the drinks while the men
Complained about their lives.

Jake never asked them questions.
He knew what he needed to know—
Men working in Lost Cabin
Had nowhere else to go.

Jake married a sheepherder's daughter,
Half-Indian, half-white.
They had two sons, and finally
Things in his life were right.

He told his boys his adventures
As a cowboy riding the plain.
"Papa," they cried, "will you take us
When you ride out again?"

One night he had an argument
With a herder named Bill Howard,
A deserter from the Border War,
A drunkard, and a coward.

"Bring over that bottle of whiskey!
If you don't grab it, I will."
"Okie said to cut you off
Until you paid your bill."

Bill Howard slammed his fist down,
"Is this some goddamn joke,
A piss-poor Mexican peon
Telling me I'm broke?"

A little after midnight
Bill came back through the door.
Three times he shot his rifle,
And Jake fell to the floor.

Then Bill beheld his triumph
As the smoke cleared from the air—
A mirror blown into splinters,
And blood splattered everywhere.

A sudden brutal outburst
No motive could explain:
One poor man killing another
Without glory, without gain.

The tales of Western heroes
Show duels in the noonday sun,
But darkness and deception
Is how most killing is done.

Father Keller came from Lander
To lay Jake in the ground.
A posse searched the mountains
Until Bill Howard was found.

There were two more graves in Wyoming
When the clover bloomed in spring.
Two strangers drifted into town
And filled the openings.

And two tall boys departed
For the cattle drives that May
With hardly a word to their mother
Who watched them ride away.

• III •

PSALM AND LAMENT FOR LOS ANGELES

I.

On the streets of Hawthorne I sat down and wept.
Yes, wept as I remembered it.

I came to the asphalt country of my childhood,
To revisit the precincts of memory.

I walked the old boulevard, where the shops
Had been condemned and demolished.

I passed the bankrupt mall, defaced and boarded.
And all was vacancy and squalor.

Where was the drugstore where my parents met?
And the neighborhood park with its Indian palms?

Where was the Plaza Theater with its neon beacon
Taller than a church spire?

I wandered the silent ruins of my city.
What was there to sing in a strange and empty land?

II.

If I forget you, Los Angeles, let my eyes burn
In the smoggy crimson of your sunsets.

If I prefer not the Queen of the Angels to other cities,
Then close my ears to the beat of your tides.

Let me stand on the piers of Malibu, blind
To the dances of the surfers and the dolphins.

But, O Los Angeles, you dash your children against the stones.
You devour your natives and your immigrants.

You destroy your father's house. You sell your daughters to strangers.
You sprawl in the carnage and count the spoils.

You stretch naked in the sunlight, beautiful and obscene—
So enormous, hungry, and impossible to pardon.

PSALM OF THE HEIGHTS

I.

You don't fall in love with Los Angeles
Until you've seen it from a distance after dark.

Up in the heights of the Hollywood Hills
You can mute the sounds and find perspective.

The pulsing anger of the traffic dissipates,
And our swank unmanageable metropolis

Dissolves with all its signage and its sewage—
Until only the radiance remains.

That's when the City of Angels appears,
Silent and weightless as a dancer's dream.

The boulevards unfold in brilliant lines.
The freeways flow like shining rivers.

The moving lights stretch into vast
And secret shapes, invisible at street level.

At the horizon, the city rises into sky,
Our demi-galaxy brighter than the zodiac.

II.

Surely our destinies are written in this zodiac,
Whose courses and conjunctions govern us.

Look down and name our starry constellations—
Wilshire, Olympic, Santa Monica.

In speeding Comets or sleek Thunderbirds,
We traveled the twelve Houses of the Heavens

Ascending Crenshaw, Sunset, or Imperial,
Locked in our private worlds of lust or laughter.

Who will cast the charts of our radiant sorrow,
Or trace the secret transits of our joy?

The traffic shimmers in its fixed trajectories,
Dense and indifferent as nebulae.

Though you resist the gaudy spectacle,
You can't escape the city's sortilege.

III.

Move away, if you wish, to the white Sierras,
Or huddle in the smoky canyons of Manhattan.

You'll miss the juvenescent rapture of LA
Where ecstasy cohabits with despair,

Lascivious and fitful as a pair of lovers.
Let someone else play grown-up.

Here the soul sings like a car radio, and no one
Asks your age because we're all immortal.

Inhale the spices of the midnight air
Drifting from Thai Town and Little Armenia.

Here on the hilltop, the city whispers to you,
"Come down and play in the traffic.

Merge into the moving lights, our myriad,
The luminous multitudes that surround you.

Join their fiery orbit. Shine with us tonight.
Where else can you become a star?"

PSALM FOR OUR LADY QUEEN OF THE ANGELS

Let us sing to our city a new song,
A song that remembers its name and its founders—
Los Pobladores, the forgotten forty-four,
Who built their pueblo beside a small river.

They named the river for the Queen of the Angels,
Nuestra Señora la Reina de los Ángeles.
Poor, they were forced to the margins of empire,
Dark, dispossessed, not one couple pure.

Let us praise the marriages and matings that created us.
Desire, swifter than democracy, merging the races—
Spanish, Aztec, African, and Anglo—
Forbidden matches made holy by children.

I praise myself, a mutt of mestizo and mezzogiorno,
The seed of exiles and violent men,
Disfigured by the burdens they shouldered to survive.
Broken or bent, their boast was their suffering.

I praise my ancestors, the unkillable poor,
The few who escaped disease or despair—
The restless, the hungry, the stubborn, the scarred.
Let us praise the dignity of their destitution.

Let us praise their mother, *Nuestra Señora*,
The lost guardian, who watches them still
From murals and medals, statues, tattoos.
She has not abandoned her divided pueblo.

She has been homeless with a hungry child,
A refugee fleeing a brutal warlord.
A mother, she held her murdered son.
Her crown is jeweled with seven sorrows.

Pray for the city that lost its name.
Pray for the people too humble for progress.
Pray for the flesh that pays for profit.
Pray for the angels kept from their queen.

Pray in the hour of our death each day
In the southern sun of our desecrated city.
Pray for us, mother of the mixed and misbegotten,
Beside our dry river and tents of the outcast poor.

• IV •

TRAVELER

Traveler, your footsteps
are the road. There's nothing more.
Traveler, there is no road,
the road is made by walking.
Walking makes the road,
and if you turn around
you only see the path
you cannot walk again.
Traveler, there is no road,
only a track of foam upon the sea.

(Antonio Machado)

AUTUMN DAY

Lord: it is time. Bright summer fades away.
Let sundials darken as your shadows grow.
Set loose your winds across the open field.

Let the last fruit still ripen on the vine,
And give the grapes a few more southern days
To warm them to perfection, and then press
Their earthy sweetness into heavy wine.

Whoever has no house now never builds one.
Whoever is alone now stays alone.
Now he will wake and read, and write long letters,
Aimlessly wandering the empty lanes,
Restless as the leaves swirling round his feet.

(Rainer Maria Rilke)

NOW YOU ARE MINE

Now you are mine. Rest with your dream inside my dream.
Love, sorrow, labor now must sleep as well.
The night revolves on its invisible wheels,
And joined to me you are as pure as sleeping amber.

No one else, my love, will ever sleep in my dreams.
You go, we go together through the waters of time.
No one else will journey through the shadows with me,
Only you, eternally alive, eternal sun, eternal moon.

Your hands unfold their delicate grip,
Their gentle gestures falling aimlessly,
Your eyes close on themselves like two gray wings,

While I follow the waters you bear which bear me away:
The night, the world, and the wind unfold their destiny,
No longer with you, I am nothing but your dream.

(Pablo Neruda)

THREE SONGS FOR HELEN SUNG

1. HOT SUMMER NIGHT

Let's go downtown. It's a hot summer night.
Lovers are sitting in sidewalk cafés—
Breaking up, making up, hooking up, cooking up
Plans for tonight that leave them amazed.

Let's go downtown. It's a hot summer night.
Let's not stay home and get in a fight.
Let's eat spicy food in a dark little dive
And let our bodies know we're alive.

Summer has come. The young are on fire,
And every tattoo spells a word for desire.
They're strolling as naked as custom allows.
They never say later. They only say now.

Let's live in the flesh and not on a screen.
Let's dress like people who want to be seen.
Don't bring me home till the dawn's early light.
Let's not waste this hot summer night.

2. BALLAD: THE STARS ON
SECOND AVENUE

I'd say it was the stars
Reminded me of you.
But I can't see the stars
From Second Avenue.
The shimmer is just neon
Reflected in the rain
From the little corner deli
Where memory comes with pain.

I'd say it was the moon
That made me lose my head.
But I never saw the moon
In the window by our bed.
It was just a streetlamp
Shining in the dark
Above the empty bench
In the empty park.

I'd say it was the wine
That eased my heavy soul.
But I never take a drink.
I never lose control.
Maybe I should blame myself,
Maybe just blame you.
The stars won't tell me anything
Here on Second Avenue.

3. TOO BAD

Too bad,
So sad.
You're such a fool
To make
Me mad.

Romance?
No chance.
Honey, you lost
Your turn
To dance.

Beg, blame.
Call my name.
Don't you know I
Won't play
Your game?

Star-crossed?
Storm-tossed?
Love your sweet words,
But now
Get lost.

In a while
Crocodile,
Your alligator tears
Just make
Me smile.

Moan, groan
On the phone.
You're gonna spend
Tonight
Alone!

YOU LEAVE ME BENT

Cabaret song

I met him last summer at the Museum of Art.
He was looking at Goyas, so I knew he was smart.
He took me to dinner. We caught a few shows.
Last week at the office, he left me a rose.
He calls me each evening for an intimate chat.
He even remembers the name of my cat.
We're madly in love, but what can I do?
Something is missing, and its color is blue.
So tonight I'm gonna tell him . . .

You leave me bent
And totally spent.
I lost my composure
The moment you went.
Why do you have
To be such a gent
And drop me off home
With zip to repent?

So impossibly handsome,
Such impeccable taste,
Each emotional test
You totally aced.
Without having laid me
You laid me to waste.
You thoroughly made me
By being so chaste.

I knew from the first
That you were a winner.
You paid for the dinner
And said I looked thinner.
I've been in your thrall
Since the day that we met.
But there's one thing
You seem to forget.

I'm rather embarrassed,
But let me be plain.
I feel like Tarzan,
So stop being Jane.
Should I bring in Cheetah
And have him explain
What the Laws of the Jungle
So clearly ordain?

You're a regular saint,
The model of virtue,
But take off your shirt.
I don't want to hurt you.
It's hard not to kick
Your gorgeous behind.
A good guy like you
Is annoying to find.

THE TREASURE SONG

The pleasures of treasure are hard to measure
When you are crowned the king.
My royal desire has been to acquire
The world's most precious thing.
Yes, the world's most precious thing.

I was told that gold was the greatest prize,
And diamonds were reckoned second.
And the case was made for silver and jade.
All of those bright things beckoned.
Oh, how those bright things beckoned.

So I gathered them all and stacked them tall,
To study them at my leisure.
But the gold was cold, and the jewels seemed small.
None of them gave me pleasure.
No, none of them gave me pleasure.

Then I found a prize that to my surprise
Surpassed all the others together,
A splendiferous, secret treasure—
Three powerful, magic feathers.
Yes, three magic feathers.

At my insistence we hid their existence,
Locked in a secret chest,
Until the hour we needed their power
To give a magical test.
Yes, to give us a magical test.

(From The Three Feathers*)*

EPITAPH

Here lies D.G. A poet? Who can say?
He didn't even have an MFA.

• V •

THE UNDERWORLD

Facilis descensus Averno
[Descending into Hell is easy.]
—VIRGIL

I. THE TRIP

It isn't difficult to visit Hell,
As long as you can follow the instructions.
Get on the Underground, the Western Line.
Go to the final car. Sit by yourself
In the last row. Don't talk to anyone.
Don't exit when you reach the outmost station.
Don't move—not even when the lights go off.

II. THE FARE

When the conductor comes to hand out tickets,
There's a small charge. No money changes hands,
But you must offer something of your own—
Your book, your fountain pen, a lock of hair,
Your smile, perhaps the memory of your mother.
He'll always notice something that he needs.
Each trade is final. There are no returns.

III. THE PASSENGERS

There will be other passengers on board.
Don't talk to them. They know much less than you.
There's nothing notable about the damned,
Except how commonplace they seem—a clerk,
An engineer, a carpenter, a thief.
And frankly, they aren't interested in you.
Sit quietly. Remember why you've come.

IV. THE PASSENGERS' PERSPECTIVE

The damned, however, likely disagree.
Perdition is a matter of perspective.
What makes them notable may not be visible.
Damnation is an essence not an outfit.
"Why this is hell, nor am I out of it,"
The instruments of pain become internal—
Barbed memory, the lash of consciousness.

V. THEIR SECRETS

Still, how can you resist surveying them—
The doctor dressed for golf, the blue-eyed girl
Who strokes the tiny scars along her arm,
The man with twenty fingers on his hand,
Or the tall bishop with his mouth sewn shut?
They sit like oracles bereft of utterance.
Theirs are the secrets Hell exists to hide.

VI. BAGGAGE

Look at the baggage everyone has brought—
Suitcases, backpacks, elegant valises
(The hand-tooled leather fragrant with adventure),
Jewelry boxes, satchels stuffed with cash,
Briefcases, laptops, thermoses, and urns—
So many needful things, so soon forgot.
Their heaviest burdens are invisible.

VII. YOUR LUGGAGE

How do you pack for an eternity?
Lightly, of course. No more than you can carry
Eternally. No wonder many choose
To wander naked. You don't plan to stay
Or bring back anything, except yourself.
Dress comfortably. Carry nothing on you,
Except a pouch of seven silver coins.

VIII. TWO RULES

Assuming you still reckon to return,
Observe these rules. Don't eat. Don't fall asleep.
Taste anything in Hell—a piece of bread,
A sip of wine, a single pumpkin seed—
And you invite the darkness into you.
Sleep, and the memories of life will fade.
You wake a dry husk turning in the wind.

IX. QUESTIONS

The travelers who ventured here before,
The living ones, who crossed into the shadows
To violate this place, could not resist
From questioning the dead. They hoped to learn
Forbidden things and yet remain untouched.
There are some truths that only darkness knows.
Such knowledge never comes without a price.

X. CONCERNING THE LEGENDS

But who can touch a web without it sticking?
The deeper they explored, the more entangled.
The truths that darkness taught infected them,
Clouding their minds, goading their descent.
A few returned, the legendary heroes.
But most remained, not searching now but lost,
No different from the shadows they had questioned.

XI. THOSE "LEGENDARY HEROES"

. . . will not include you. You abjure heroics.
No epic journey, just a private trip
Without ambition for reward or glory.
You cross the border between worlds to bring
Belated gifts to your uneasy dead.
No winged divinity spoke in your dreams.
Nothing compels you but your riven heart.

XII. THE QUESTION

The question should be asked—why have you come?
Why willingly depart the rain, the stars,
The gold abundance of the morning sky,
The dusty ripeness of the apple bough?
The question should be asked—but no one speaks.
The train jogs forward through the dark. You learn
No one will stop you on the journey down.

XIII. THE VIEW

Tunnels at first, then at long intervals
More subway platforms—dim and dirty stations
No longer used, it seems, by anyone
Except the dead. More passengers get on.
But no one leaves. The doors close with a hiss.
The train car shudders as it gathers speed—
Going nowhere but going very fast.

XIV. INTO THE UNDERWORLD

The train emerges to a lowland plain
Bordered by mountains on either side.
Behind each range another range arises,
Higher and curving inward like a dome—
A space at once enormous and confined,
Not dark but dim and shadowed like the twilight,
A landscape without sky, an underworld.

XV. COMPOSURE

How calm you are. With such urbane composure
You notice that the woman next to you
Has turned to stone. Strange, but she now seems more
Beautiful in her alabaster skin,
So delicately weathered by the years.
No sudden Gorgon-gaze arrested her.
She drew this slow perfection from within.

XVI. APPROACHING THE CITY

A trembling passes through the crowded car
As the dark city rises in the distance.
Even the damned are anxious to arrive.
They fumble with their baggage nervously.
Surely some revelation is at hand.
This world can't be as indecipherable
As the last. Hell at least must offer order.

XVII. DISAPPOINTMENTS

No fire, no furies, no ferryman,
No bleeding thorns, no waters of oblivion,
No triple-headed dog to guard the gate,
No gate at all as far as you can tell,
No burning wheel, no stones to push uphill,
No Titans bound in chains, no serpent king.
No sun, no moon, no stars, no sky, no end.

NOTES ON THE POEMS

Meet Me at the Lighthouse

Jazz fans will recognize the names of the ghosts sitting in with the Lighthouse All-Stars—Gerry Mulligan, Cannonball Adderley, Hampton Hawes, Stan Getz, Chet Baker, and Art Pepper. Tartarus is the abyss of the Underworld. The poem is addressed to my cousin Philip Dragotto who died at thirty-nine.

Pardon Me, Pilgrim

Locally called a luna moth, this insect is actually a polyphemus moth. As big as an outstretched hand, it has wings that mimic the eyes of an owl.

Seaward

All three of my Ortiz uncles joined the US Merchant Marine as teenagers and served during World War II. The youngest, Theodore Ortiz, remained in the service until his early death.

"Words, Words, Words"

The title comes from Hamlet's reply to Polonius's question, "What do you read, my lord?"

The Ballad of Jesús Ortiz

"The Ballad of Jesús Ortiz" describes the life and death of my great-grandfather. Every name, place, and significant event is true. The ballad has traditionally been the form to document the stories of the poor, particularly in the Old West. The people remembered in the poem would have sung ballads and *corridos*. The form seemed the right way to tell their story.

Three Songs for Helen Sung

These lyrics were written for jazz pianist and composer Helen Sung who set them in her album *Sung with Words* (2018).

The Treasure Song

"The Treasure Song" is performed by the slightly mad old king in Lori Laitman's fairy tale opera *The Three Feathers*.

The Underworld

This sequence makes allusions to Virgil, Seneca, Dante, Christopher Marlowe, W. B. Yeats, and T. S. Eliot as well as Kelly Link and Clive Barker.

ACKNOWLEDGMENTS

These poems, sometimes in significantly different versions, appeared in *Alta, America, American Scholar, Catamaran, Dark Horse, Evansville Review, First Things, Hudson Review, Los Angeles Review of Books, Modern Age, New Criterion, Poetry South, Rattle,* and *Virginia Quarterly Review.*

"Meet Me at the Lighthouse" was reprinted in *The Best American Poetry 2016,* edited by Edward Hirsch. It also appeared in *Trading Eights: The Faces of Jazz,* a folio of engravings by James G. Todd Jr. (Mixolydian Editions, 2016).

"The Ballad of Jesús Ortiz" and "Psalms and Lament for Los Angeles" appeared in letterpress editions from Providence Press.

"Epitaph" appeared as part of the final book of Aralia Press.

The translation of Pablo Neruda's "Now You Are Mine" was done for composer Morten Lauridsen. "You Leave Me Bent" was written as a cabaret song for composer Lori Laitman. "The Treasure Song" is from the libretto of *The Three Feathers,* a fairy tale opera also written for the composer Lori Laitman.

DANA GIOIA was born in Los Angeles in 1950. He received his BA and MBA degrees from Stanford University. He also has an MA in Comparative Literature from Harvard University. For fifteen years, he worked as a business executive in New York before quitting in 1992 to write full-time. He has published five earlier collections of poetry—*Daily Horoscope* (1986), *The Gods of Winter* (1991), *Interrogations at Noon* (2001), which won the American Book Award, *Pity the Beautiful* (2012), and *99 Poems: New and Selected* (2016), which won the Poets' Prize. Gioia's first critical collection, *Can Poetry Matter?* (1992), was a finalist for the National Book Critics Circle Award. Gioia has received the Laetare Medal from Notre Dame University and the Aiken Taylor Award in Modern American Poetry. From 2003 to 2009, he served as Chairman of the National Endowment for the Arts. An essayist, reviewer, and translator, Gioia has also edited fifteen anthologies of poetry and fiction. He is the former Poet Laureate of California. He divides his time between Los Angeles and Sonoma County, California.

The text of *Meet Me at the Lighthouse* is set in Galliard Pro type and was based on a design by Tree Swenson. Composition by Bookmobile Design & Digital Publisher Services, Minneapolis, Minnesota. Manufactured by Versa Press on acid-free, 30 percent postconsumer wastepaper.